EMMANUEL JOSEPH

Rhapsody of Holistic Prosperity, Crafting a Balanced Life through Wealth, Wellness, and Connection

Copyright © 2025 by Emmanuel Joseph

All rights reserved. No part of this publication may be reproduced, stored or transmitted in any form or by any means, electronic, mechanical, photocopying, recording, scanning, or otherwise without written permission from the publisher. It is illegal to copy this book, post it to a website, or distribute it by any other means without permission.

First edition

This book was professionally typeset on Reedsy. Find out more at reedsy.com

Contents

1. Chapter 1: The Journey Begins — 1
2. Chapter 2: Redefining Wealth — 3
3. Chapter 3: Wellness from Within — 5
4. Chapter 4: Cultivating Connection — 7
5. Chapter 5: The Power of Purpose — 9
6. Chapter 6: Financial Literacy and Freedom — 10
7. Chapter 7: Health as Wealth — 12
8. Chapter 8: Mindfulness and Mental Clarity — 14
9. Chapter 9: Emotional Intelligence — 16
10. Chapter 10: Lifelong Learning — 18
11. Chapter 11: The Art of Giving — 20
12. Chapter 12: Sustainable Living — 22
13. Chapter 13: Building Resilience — 24
14. Chapter 14: The Harmony of Work and Play — 26
15. Chapter 15: Crafting a Legacy — 28

1

Chapter 1: The Journey Begins

Embarking on the journey to holistic prosperity requires introspection and understanding of what truly matters. Prosperity is often misinterpreted as mere financial success, but it encompasses much more. True prosperity integrates wealth, wellness, and meaningful connections into a balanced and fulfilling life. It starts with recognizing one's core values, setting purposeful goals, and aligning daily actions with these objectives. By redefining what it means to be prosperous, one can begin to carve a path toward a life rich in all dimensions.

The first step in this journey is to pause and reflect. Take the time to evaluate your current state of life—what brings you joy, what drains your energy, and what areas need attention. This self-assessment serves as a foundation for setting intentional goals that align with your values. Remember, holistic prosperity is not about achieving perfection but about striving for balance and growth.

As you embark on this path, it is essential to cultivate a mindset of abundance. Abundance thinking focuses on possibilities, opportunities, and gratitude. It shifts the perspective from scarcity and lack to one of potential and fulfillment. By adopting an abundance mindset, you create a fertile ground for growth in all aspects of life.

Lastly, surround yourself with a supportive network. Seek out mentors, friends, and communities that inspire and uplift you. The journey to holistic prosperity is not meant to be traveled alone. Together, you can share insights, celebrate successes, and navigate challenges, making the experience richer and more rewarding.

Let's continue with Chapter 2:

2

Chapter 2: Redefining Wealth

Wealth is often synonymous with money, but it extends beyond financial gains. Wealth includes time, energy, knowledge, relationships, and experiences. By broadening the definition of wealth, individuals can appreciate the full spectrum of their assets. Wealth accumulation then becomes a multidimensional endeavor, where investments in personal growth, health, and community hold as much importance as monetary investments. This holistic approach to wealth fosters a more sustainable and satisfying life.

Financial wealth is undoubtedly important, but it should not be the sole focus. Consider the value of time and how it is spent. Time is a finite resource, and using it wisely can lead to greater fulfillment. Invest time in activities that nurture your well-being, strengthen relationships, and contribute to personal growth.

Energy is another critical component of wealth. Maintaining high energy levels allows you to pursue your goals with vigor and enthusiasm. Prioritize activities and habits that boost your energy, such as regular exercise, healthy eating, and adequate rest. By managing your energy effectively, you can maximize productivity and enjoyment in all areas of life.

Knowledge and skills are invaluable assets that contribute to overall wealth. Continuously seek opportunities to learn and grow, whether through formal education, workshops, or self-study. Knowledge enhances your ability to make informed decisions, solve problems, and innovate. It empowers you to navigate the complexities of life with confidence and competence.

Lastly, cherish and nurture your relationships. Meaningful connections provide emotional support, joy, and a sense of belonging. Invest time and effort into building and maintaining strong relationships with family, friends, and community. These connections enrich your life and contribute to your overall sense of prosperity.

3

Chapter 3: Wellness from Within

Wellness is the cornerstone of holistic prosperity. It begins with self-care and extends to physical, emotional, and mental well-being. True wellness is achieved by balancing these aspects and nurturing oneself with healthy habits, positive thoughts, and regular exercise. Additionally, mindfulness practices, such as meditation and journaling, play a crucial role in maintaining inner peace. By prioritizing wellness, individuals can harness the energy and resilience needed to pursue their goals.

Physical wellness involves maintaining a healthy body through proper nutrition, regular exercise, and adequate rest. A balanced diet, rich in nutrients, fuels the body and supports overall health. Physical activity, whether through structured workouts or enjoyable activities like dancing or hiking, keeps the body strong and agile. Sufficient sleep is essential for recovery and rejuvenation, allowing the body and mind to function optimally.

Emotional wellness is about understanding and managing emotions. It involves developing a positive self-image, coping with stress, and nurturing relationships. Practices such as gratitude, self-compassion, and emotional expression contribute to emotional health. By acknowledging and addressing emotions, individuals can build resilience and maintain a balanced emotional state.

Mental wellness focuses on cognitive functions and mental clarity. Engaging in intellectually stimulating activities, such as reading, puzzles, or learning new skills, keeps the mind sharp. Mindfulness practices, such as meditation and deep breathing, enhance mental clarity and reduce stress. By prioritizing mental wellness, individuals can improve focus, decision-making, and overall cognitive health.

Let's continue with Chapter 4:

4

Chapter 4: Cultivating Connection

Human connections are the threads that weave the fabric of a prosperous life. Meaningful relationships provide support, joy, and a sense of belonging. Cultivating deep connections requires empathy, active listening, and genuine care for others. By investing time and effort into relationships, individuals can build a strong network of family, friends, and community. These connections enhance well-being and offer a support system through life's challenges and triumphs.

Building strong relationships involves being present and attentive. Active listening, where one truly hears and understands the other person, fosters deeper connections. Empathy, the ability to understand and share the feelings of others, strengthens bonds. Genuine care and kindness create a supportive and nurturing environment.

Nurturing relationships also means setting healthy boundaries and maintaining balance. It is essential to recognize and respect one's own needs while being considerate of others. Healthy relationships are built on mutual respect, trust, and open communication. By fostering these qualities, individuals can create lasting and meaningful connections.

Community involvement is another vital aspect of cultivating connection. Engaging with local organizations, volunteering, or participating in community events fosters a sense of belonging and purpose. It provides opportunities to meet new people, share experiences, and contribute to the greater good.

By being an active member of the community, individuals can enhance their overall well-being and create a positive impact.

5

Chapter 5: The Power of Purpose

Living a life of purpose is essential for holistic prosperity. Purpose provides direction, motivation, and a sense of fulfillment. It involves identifying one's passions, strengths, and how they can be used to contribute to the greater good. By aligning daily activities with a greater purpose, individuals can experience a profound sense of meaning and satisfaction. Purpose-driven living transforms mundane tasks into meaningful endeavors, creating a life rich with intent and impact.

Identifying purpose begins with self-reflection. Consider what brings joy, passion, and a sense of accomplishment. Reflect on past experiences, strengths, and values to uncover what truly matters. Purpose is not static; it can evolve over time as one grows and gains new insights.

Once identified, purpose becomes a guiding force in daily life. It influences decisions, priorities, and actions. Purpose-driven living involves setting goals that align with one's purpose and taking consistent steps toward achieving them. It requires resilience, perseverance, and a commitment to personal growth.

Purpose also extends beyond the self. It involves contributing to the well-being of others and making a positive impact on the world. Acts of kindness, service, and advocacy contribute to a greater sense of purpose. By living with purpose, individuals can create a life that is not only prosperous but also meaningful and fulfilling.

6

Chapter 6: Financial Literacy and Freedom

Financial literacy is a critical component of prosperity. Understanding personal finance, budgeting, investing, and managing debt empowers individuals to make informed decisions. Financial freedom is achieved by building a solid financial foundation, minimizing liabilities, and creating multiple streams of income. This freedom allows for greater flexibility and the ability to pursue passions without the constraints of financial stress. Financial literacy is an ongoing journey, requiring continuous learning and adaptation.

Financial literacy begins with understanding the basics of personal finance. This includes creating and sticking to a budget, tracking expenses, and setting financial goals. A budget helps manage income and expenses, ensuring that resources are allocated effectively. Tracking expenses provides insight into spending habits and areas for improvement.

Investing is another crucial aspect of financial literacy. It involves putting money into assets that have the potential to grow over time, such as stocks, bonds, real estate, or mutual funds. Understanding the principles of investing, such as risk and return, diversification, and compounding, empowers individuals to make informed investment decisions.

Managing debt is also essential for financial freedom. It involves understanding the types of debt, interest rates, and repayment strategies. Minimizing high-interest debt and managing credit responsibly contribute to financial stability. By maintaining a healthy balance of debt and credit, individuals can avoid financial stress and build a solid financial foundation.

Financial literacy is a lifelong journey that requires continuous learning and adaptation. Staying informed about financial trends, seeking advice from financial professionals, and staying disciplined in financial habits are key to achieving and maintaining financial freedom.

7

Chapter 7: Health as Wealth

Health is the most valuable asset one can possess. It is the foundation upon which all other aspects of prosperity are built. Maintaining good health involves a balanced diet, regular exercise, sufficient sleep, and preventive care. A proactive approach to health ensures longevity and vitality, enabling individuals to fully enjoy their wealth and relationships. By prioritizing health, one can live a vibrant and active life, free from the limitations of illness.

A balanced diet is essential for good health. It involves consuming a variety of nutrient-rich foods, including fruits, vegetables, whole grains, lean proteins, and healthy fats. Proper nutrition provides the body with the energy and nutrients needed to function optimally and prevent chronic diseases.

Regular exercise is also crucial for maintaining health. Physical activity helps maintain a healthy weight, improves cardiovascular health, strengthens muscles and bones, and enhances mental well-being. Finding enjoyable ways to stay active, such as walking, swimming, or dancing, makes it easier to incorporate exercise into daily routines.

Adequate sleep is vital for overall health and well-being. It allows the body to rest, recover, and repair. Quality sleep improves cognitive function, mood, and immune system function. Establishing a consistent sleep schedule and creating a relaxing bedtime routine can help improve sleep quality.

Preventive care involves regular check-ups, screenings, and vaccinations to detect and prevent health issues before they become serious. By staying proactive about health, individuals can catch potential problems early and take steps to address them. Preventive care also includes managing stress, practicing good hygiene, and avoiding harmful behaviors such as smoking and excessive alcohol consumption.

8

Chapter 8: Mindfulness and Mental Clarity

Mindfulness is the practice of being present and fully engaged in the moment. It fosters mental clarity, reduces stress, and enhances overall well-being. Techniques such as meditation, deep breathing, and mindful movement help cultivate mindfulness. By incorporating these practices into daily routines, individuals can improve focus, emotional regulation, and resilience. Mindfulness creates a sense of inner calm, allowing for more thoughtful and deliberate actions.

Mindfulness begins with paying attention to the present moment without judgment. It involves observing thoughts, feelings, and sensations as they arise, without getting caught up in them. This awareness helps individuals respond to situations with greater clarity and composure.

Meditation is a powerful tool for cultivating mindfulness. It involves sitting quietly and focusing on the breath or a specific object, allowing thoughts to come and go without attachment. Regular meditation practice enhances concentration, reduces stress, and promotes a sense of inner peace.

Deep breathing exercises also contribute to mindfulness. Taking slow, deep breaths calms the nervous system and brings attention to the present moment. Deep breathing can be practiced anytime, anywhere, to manage stress and enhance focus.

CHAPTER 8: MINDFULNESS AND MENTAL CLARITY

Mindful movement, such as yoga or tai chi, combines physical activity with mindful awareness. These practices involve paying attention to the body's movements, sensations, and alignment, promoting a sense of balance and harmony. Mindful movement enhances physical and mental well-being, making it an excellent addition to a holistic wellness routine.

9

Chapter 9: Emotional Intelligence

Emotional intelligence is the ability to understand and manage one's emotions, as well as empathize with others. It is a crucial skill for building strong relationships and navigating life's challenges. Developing emotional intelligence involves self-awareness, self-regulation, motivation, empathy, and social skills. By enhancing these abilities, individuals can improve communication, conflict resolution, and overall emotional well-being. Emotional intelligence is a key component of a balanced and prosperous life.

Self-awareness is the foundation of emotional intelligence. It involves recognizing and understanding one's emotions, strengths, weaknesses, and triggers. Self-awareness allows individuals to respond to situations with greater insight and intention.

Self-regulation involves managing emotions in a healthy and constructive way. It includes techniques such as deep breathing, positive self-talk, and mindfulness to stay calm and composed. By practicing self-regulation, individuals can navigate stressful situations with resilience and grace.

Motivation is the drive to pursue goals with passion and perseverance. It involves setting meaningful goals, maintaining a positive attitude, and staying committed to personal growth. Motivation fuels progress and achievement, contributing to overall well-being.

Empathy is the ability to understand and share the feelings of others. It involves active listening, open-mindedness, and genuine concern for others. Empathy strengthens relationships and fosters a sense of connection and understanding.

Social skills are the tools used to interact effectively with others. These include communication, collaboration, conflict resolution, and leadership. By honing social skills, individuals can build strong relationships, work effectively in teams, and navigate social dynamics with ease.

10

Chapter 10: Lifelong Learning

Lifelong learning is the continuous pursuit of knowledge and personal growth. It involves staying curious, open-minded, and committed to self-improvement. Whether through formal education, workshops, or self-study, lifelong learning keeps the mind sharp and adaptable. It fosters innovation, creativity, and resilience in the face of change. By embracing lifelong learning, individuals can stay relevant, fulfilled, and equipped to seize new opportunities.

Staying curious is the first step toward lifelong learning. Curiosity drives exploration and discovery, leading to new insights and experiences. It involves asking questions, seeking answers, and being open to new ideas and perspectives.

Formal education, such as enrolling in courses or obtaining certifications, provides structured learning opportunities. It allows individuals to deepen their knowledge in specific areas and gain valuable credentials. However, learning is not confined to formal education; self-study, reading, and hands-on experiences are equally valuable.

Workshops and seminars offer opportunities for skill-building and networking. They provide a platform to learn from experts, engage in discussions, and share knowledge with peers. By participating in workshops, individuals can stay updated on industry trends and expand their professional networks.

CHAPTER 10: LIFELONG LEARNING

Self-study involves taking charge of one's learning journey. It includes reading books, watching educational videos, and practicing new skills. Self-study allows individuals to learn at their own pace and tailor their learning experience to their interests and goals.

11

Chapter 11: The Art of Giving

Giving is a fundamental aspect of holistic prosperity. It involves sharing time, resources, and talents with others. Acts of generosity, whether big or small, create a ripple effect of positive impact. Giving fosters a sense of community, gratitude, and purpose. It strengthens relationships and enhances overall well-being. By making giving a regular practice, individuals can contribute to a better world and experience the joy of making a difference.

Giving time is one of the most valuable forms of generosity. Volunteering, mentoring, or simply being present for others makes a significant impact. Time is a precious resource, and giving it to others shows care and commitment.

Sharing resources, such as money, food, or clothing, helps meet the needs of others. Donations to charities, supporting local businesses, or helping a neighbor in need are all ways to share resources. Acts of kindness, no matter how small, can make a meaningful difference.

Using talents to give back is another powerful way to contribute. Skills and expertise can be used to teach, inspire, and support others. Whether it's offering pro bono services, sharing knowledge, or creating something of value, using talents to give back enriches both the giver and the receiver.

Gratitude and appreciation are integral to the art of giving. Recognizing and expressing gratitude for what one has fosters a positive mindset and encourages further generosity. It creates a cycle of giving and receiving that enhances overall well-being.

12

Chapter 12: Sustainable Living

Sustainable living is about making choices that support the well-being of the planet and future generations. It involves reducing waste, conserving resources, and embracing eco-friendly practices. Sustainable living extends to all areas of life, including consumption, transportation, and energy use. By adopting sustainable habits, individuals can reduce their environmental footprint and contribute to a healthier planet. Sustainability is an integral part of holistic prosperity, ensuring the longevity of resources for future generations.

Reducing waste is a key aspect of sustainable living. This involves minimizing single-use plastics, recycling, and reusing items whenever possible. By being mindful of waste, individuals can lessen their impact on the environment and promote a culture of sustainability.

Conserving resources, such as water and energy, is another important practice. Simple actions, like turning off lights when not in use, fixing leaks, and using energy-efficient appliances, contribute to resource conservation. Sustainable transportation options, such as walking, biking, or using public transport, also reduce carbon emissions.

Embracing eco-friendly practices involves choosing products and services that have a minimal environmental impact. This includes supporting companies with sustainable practices, using biodegradable products, and opting for plant-based diets. By making conscious choices, individuals can

CHAPTER 12: SUSTAINABLE LIVING

support a more sustainable economy.

Sustainable living also extends to community involvement. Participating in local environmental initiatives, advocating for green policies, and educating others about sustainability contribute to collective efforts for a healthier planet. By working together, communities can create a positive impact and foster a culture of sustainability.

13

Chapter 13: Building Resilience

Resilience is the ability to bounce back from adversity and maintain a positive outlook. It is a crucial trait for navigating life's challenges and achieving long-term success. Building resilience involves developing coping strategies, maintaining a support network, and cultivating a growth mindset. Resilient individuals view setbacks as opportunities for learning and growth. By embracing resilience, individuals can persevere through difficulties and emerge stronger, more capable, and more prosperous.

Developing coping strategies is essential for building resilience. These strategies may include problem-solving, seeking support, practicing self-care, and managing stress. By having a toolkit of coping mechanisms, individuals can navigate challenges with greater ease.

Maintaining a support network is also vital. Surrounding oneself with supportive friends, family, and mentors provides a safety net during tough times. These connections offer emotional support, guidance, and encouragement, helping individuals stay resilient.

Cultivating a growth mindset involves viewing challenges as opportunities for learning and growth. It means embracing change, staying adaptable, and being open to new experiences. A growth mindset fosters resilience by encouraging individuals to see setbacks as temporary and surmountable.

Practicing self-care is another important aspect of resilience. Taking time to relax, recharge, and nurture oneself is essential for maintaining physical, emotional, and mental well-being. Self-care activities, such as exercise, meditation, hobbies, and spending time in nature, contribute to overall resilience.

14

Chapter 14: The Harmony of Work and Play

Achieving a balance between work and play is essential for holistic prosperity. It involves setting boundaries, managing time effectively, and prioritizing self-care. A harmonious balance ensures that work responsibilities are met without sacrificing personal well-being. It allows for leisure, hobbies, and relaxation, which are crucial for overall happiness and productivity. By finding harmony between work and play, individuals can lead a balanced and fulfilling life.

Setting boundaries is the first step toward achieving balance. This involves clearly defining work hours, personal time, and family time. By setting boundaries, individuals can protect their personal well-being and ensure that work does not encroach on other areas of life.

Managing time effectively is also crucial. This includes prioritizing tasks, delegating when necessary, and avoiding overcommitment. Time management techniques, such as creating to-do lists, using calendars, and setting deadlines, help individuals stay organized and focused.

Prioritizing self-care is essential for maintaining balance. This includes taking regular breaks, engaging in enjoyable activities, and ensuring adequate rest. Self-care activities, such as exercise, hobbies, and socializing, contribute to overall well-being and prevent burnout.

CHAPTER 14: THE HARMONY OF WORK AND PLAY

Leisure and hobbies play a vital role in achieving harmony. Engaging in activities that bring joy and relaxation provides a break from work and fosters creativity and happiness. Whether it's reading, gardening, painting, or playing sports, hobbies enrich life and contribute to a balanced lifestyle.

15

Chapter 15: Crafting a Legacy

Crafting a legacy is about leaving a lasting impact on the world. It involves intentional actions that contribute to the well-being of others and the planet. A legacy is built through positive contributions, meaningful relationships, and a life lived with purpose. It reflects the values, achievements, and influence of an individual. By focusing on creating a legacy, individuals can ensure that their efforts and experiences resonate beyond their lifetime, inspiring future generations to pursue holistic prosperity.

Legacy begins with living a life of integrity and purpose. It involves aligning actions with values and making meaningful contributions to society. Whether through career achievements, community involvement, or acts of kindness, every positive action contributes to one's legacy.

Building meaningful relationships is also a crucial part of crafting a legacy. The impact one has on family, friends, colleagues, and the community shapes how one is remembered. By fostering positive and supportive relationships, individuals create a lasting influence that extends beyond their lifetime.

Contributing to the well-being of others and the planet is another aspect of legacy. This includes acts of service, philanthropy, and advocacy for social and environmental causes. By making a positive difference, individuals leave a mark that benefits future generations.

Reflecting on the impact one wants to leave helps guide actions and

CHAPTER 15: CRAFTING A LEGACY

decisions. It encourages individuals to live with purpose, make intentional choices, and strive for meaningful accomplishments.

Epilogue: The Symphony of a Balanced Life Holistic prosperity is a symphony of wealth, wellness, and connection. It requires intentionality, balance, and a commitment to continuous growth. By embracing the principles outlined in this book, individuals can craft a life that resonates with harmony, fulfillment, and lasting impact. The journey to holistic prosperity is a personal and evolving one, but it is ultimately a path to a richer, more balanced, and meaningful existence.

Book Description:

Rhapsody of Holistic Prosperity: Crafting a Balanced Life through Wealth, Wellness, and Connection is a transformative guide to achieving true prosperity. This insightful book redefines prosperity beyond mere financial success, integrating wealth, wellness, and meaningful connections into a harmonious and fulfilling life.

Embark on a journey of self-discovery and growth as you explore the principles of holistic prosperity. Each chapter delves into essential aspects of a balanced life, from redefining wealth and prioritizing wellness to cultivating deep connections and living with purpose. Discover the importance of financial literacy, lifelong learning, sustainable living, and building resilience. Learn the art of giving, achieving work-life harmony, and crafting a lasting legacy.

This book offers practical advice, thoughtful insights, and actionable steps to help you create a life rich in all dimensions. Whether you seek personal growth, improved well-being, or a deeper sense of fulfillment, *Rhapsody of Holistic Prosperity* provides the tools and inspiration to craft a prosperous and meaningful life. Join the journey to holistic prosperity and unlock the true potential of a balanced and enriched existence.

www.ingramcontent.com/pod-product-compliance
Lightning Source LLC
LaVergne TN
LVHW010444070526
838199LV00066B/6180